TABLE OF CONTENTS

RIGHT NOW I NEED FAITH

My Father Is Always at Work 6
Follow Me 9

RIGHT NOW I NEED PATIENCE

The Lord Is My Portion 13
Is Anything Too Hard for the Lord? 16

RIGHT NOW I NEED TRUST

Blessed Are Those Who Trust in the Lord .. 20
If You Believe, You Will See 23

RIGHT NOW I NEED HOPE

How Long, Lord? 27
I Still Dare to Hope 30

RIGHT NOW I NEED PEACE

Let the Peace of God Rule Your Heart 34
Why Do You Hide Yourself, Lord? 37

RIGHT NOW I NEED BALANCE

Lord, You Alone Are My Portion 41
Seek First the Kingdom 44

RIGHT NOW I NEED PERSPECTIVE

A New Name 48
Intended for Good 51

RIGHT NOW I NEED CONTENTMENT

Never Thirst Again 55
Forget Not His Benefits 58

RIGHT NOW I NEED PERSEVERANCE

We Never Give Up 62
The Will of Him Who Sent Me 65

RIGHT NOW I NEED REASSURANCE

The Way of the Righteous 69
A Sure and Steadfast Anchor 72

and it will be given to you; seek, and you will find; knock, and it will be opened to you. For everyone who asks receives, and the one who seeks finds, and to the one who knocks it will be opened. Or which one of you, if his son asks him for bread, will give him a stone? Or if he asks for a fish, will give him a serpent? If you then, who are evil, know how to give good gifts to your children, how much more will your Father who is in heaven give good things to those who ask him!

MATTHEW 7:7–11 (ESV)

FORGET ABOUT THE REST OF THE YEAR FOR A SECOND.

Forget about the month.

Forget about the week.

Now forget about what you have to do by tomorrow, then about what you have to do in the next couple of hours.

Think about this moment — right now.

How are you feeling? Are you stressed because you feel like you need to be everywhere at once? Are you still reeling from that hurtful thing said to you? Do you feel like you're about to lose your mind because nothing — *nothing* — is going according to plan?

This book is filled with reminders of who you may have lost sight of in the midst of today, someone we all lose sight of sometimes: Jesus.

As you read through these devotions, remember that Jesus is the giver of all these gifts. Matthew 7:11 says, "If you then, who are evil, know how to give good gifts to your children, how much more will your Father who is in heaven give good things to those who ask him!" (ESV)

At the end of each devotion, there will be a space for you to write one thing down you know to be true. Use those lines as a way to encourage yourself in what you're currently facing. Then, when you need to refer back to that page, your own words will serve as a reminder!

Faith. Hope. Reassurance. Patience. Whatever it is you need at this very moment, you can ask Him, the giver of all good gifts, and He will gladly give it to you.

Blessed is the man

who walks not in the counsel of the wicked,

nor stands in the way of sinners,

nor sits in the seat of scoffers;

but his delight is in the law of the Lord,

and on his law he meditates day and night.

He is like a tree

planted by streams of water

that yields its fruit in its season,

and its leaf does not wither.

In all that he does, he prospers.

PSALM 1:1–3

right now I need

FAITH

MY FATHER IS ALWAYS AT WORK

"Jesus said, 'My Father is always at his work to this very day, and I too am working.'" John 5:17 (NIV)

In 1 Kings 18:41-45, there's a story about a prophet named Elijah. God had caused a three-and-a-half-year drought in Israel because His people followed foreign gods. Miracle after miracle occurred during those years, but it's what happened at the end of the drought that may catch your attention.

Elijah sent a message to King Ahab to let him know that the 42-month dry spell was coming to an end, even though there wasn't a cloud in the sky. After delivering the news, Elijah climbed to the top of Carmel, bent down to the ground and put his face between his knees.

"'Go and look toward the sea,' he told his servant" (1 Kings 18:43a NIV). He wanted him to see if there was a cloud.

"There's nothing there," (1 Kings 18:43b NIV) the servant said upon his return. Six times Elijah sent the servant back down the mountain to see if there was a cloud. Six times he returned reporting there was not.

Elijah said a seventh time, "Go back" (v. 43).

Based on "When You Feel Like Prayer Isn't Working" by Sharon Jaynes

He observed the sky and came back to tell Elijah the news, "A cloud as small as a man's hand is rising from the sea" (1 Kings 18:44b NIV).

If you remember anything about rain cycles from elementary school, you might recall that water falls from the sky into oceans, rivers and lakes. The sun heats the water, and it evaporates as water vapor. The vapor rises from the earth into the atmosphere, cools, then forms droplets called condensation.

Little droplets get together and form bigger droplets. Eventually those droplets form clouds. When the droplets get too heavy, they fall back to the earth as precipitation into oceans, rivers and lakes. Then the cycle starts all over again.

God was working during the servant's first run down the mountain; the servant just couldn't see it. As Jesus said, "My Father is always at his work to this very day, and I too am working" (John 5:17). Just because you can't see God working doesn't mean He's not.

No matter what you're praying about today, don't give up. God is always working ... even if we can't see it.

Based on "When You Feel Like Prayer Isn't Working" by Sharon Jaynes

In the space below, write one thing you know to be true based off what you read today:

God is at work, even when I can't see it.
- Is this because we can't see the future?
- In retrospect, I see how He has worked even when I thought nothing was happening.
- So then, why is faith such a difficult thing? Perhaps because life is hard and something inside us thinks it shouldn't be.

FOLLOW ME

"The next day Jesus decided to leave for Galilee. Finding Philip, he said to him, 'Follow me.'" John 1:43 (NIV)

A flashlight is a great tool. If you've ever used one camping or when your power went out, you know that during those times a little light can be invaluable.

But a flashlight isn't the same as daylight — it doesn't give us the ability to see the entire path, just enough to take one or two steps. And when you can only see one step ahead of you, it's easy to get anxious.

Taking the next step is something Jesus recommended a very long time ago. "Come and you will see." "Follow me." These were the words Jesus spoke to the disciples as He called them. He didn't sit them down and reveal what the next three years would hold. He knew they would be overwhelmed, possibly even turn around. He chose to keep it simple: "Follow me" was all He said. Take the next step …

We all wonder about our future sometimes. Will all my dreams come true? What college will I attend? What career path do I take? Will my kids be alright? Will my husband find the right job? Jesus knows the answers to your questions. But, in wisdom, He will only reveal enough light for you to take the next step.

Based on "But I Can't See!" by Lynn Cowell

Jesus knows. He knows which answers are "yes" and which ones are "no." He knows when and where to reveal to you your next step. Your part is simply to take the next step in obedience.

You'll learn that when He says "no," it's often a stepping stone to His amazing "yes." When you step forward in trust and obedience, blessing is down the path. And even those pathways that held pain were part of the process. They will be stepping stones in your journey of choosing obedience over worry, fear and control.

Now, when fear and doubt surface in the dark ... silence the "what ifs." Remember Jesus' words, "Follow me," and get back on the path that is flickering just ahead. Simply take the next step — a step of trust. Ask Him what you need to do for just today. Walk away from worry by expressing your concerns to Jesus and trust His ability to take care of each and every step.

Based on "But I Can't See!" by Lynn Cowell

In the space below, write one thing you know to be true based off what you read today:

right now I need

PATIENCE

THE LORD IS MY PORTION

"I say to myself, 'The Lord is my portion; therefore I will wait for him.'" Lamentations 3:24 (NIV)

Do you like waiting? Standing in line at the grocery store, sitting in a waiting room at the dentist's office, lingering at the airport or anxiously waiting to board your plane — does any of that sound like fun? Probably not.

While these types of hindrances are short-lived, waiting for the next big thing can take longer and be harder. We wait on Prince Charming to appear, our house to sell, our child to take their first steps, a better job, financial relief, or physical or emotional healing to come for us or a loved one.

Instead of patiently embracing these harder times, we all have a tendency to want to rush them. We long for our circumstances to hurry up and change. To fast-forward to the next thing. But Scripture teaches us how to make it through these difficult seasons.

In those waiting times, even when life is hard, God says to us, "I'll be what you need while you wait."

God steps in to be our portion for that day. He is in the wait, and we'll sense that, if only we will look for Him rather than always looking ahead to the next stage of life.

Based on "Embrace the Wait" by Karen Ehman

The point of life is not to keep looking ahead, but to look to the Lord to be our portion at every stage of life. Will you seek Him as you sit and wait? It makes the lingering have meaning and tethers our hearts to His as we use these times to pray and ponder His goodness. Yes, right in the midst of those in-between times. It even makes the waiting sweeter.

In the space below, write one thing you know to be true based off what you read today:

IS ANYTHING TOO HARD FOR THE LORD?

"Is anything too hard for the Lord? I will return to you at the appointed time next year, and Sarah will have a son." Genesis 18:14 (NIV)

Have you ever gotten stuck behind a slow driver when you were in a rush to get somewhere? It never seems to get less irritating. At some point you just want to scream through your windshield, "Hurry! Hurry! HURRY!"

How many times have we approached God's timing the same way? God rarely operates at a pace that satisfies us, and we want Him to hurry, hurry, hurry!

There was a woman in the Bible who felt past her prime and also had trouble with God's timing. Sarah, Abraham's wife, felt impatient just like we feel impatient sometimes. After waiting 10 years for the baby God had promised her (Genesis 12-21), Sarah decided to help God hurry. *Surely 10 years was too long for anybody to wait,* she likely reasoned. So she gave her maidservant Hagar to her husband, and the two of them had a child. But it turned out "helping" didn't help, and the promise still wasn't fulfilled.

Fourteen years later, Sarah and Abraham had a visitor who reminded them of God's promise, causing Sarah to laugh out loud and say, "After I am worn out and my lord is old, will I now have this pleasure?" (Genesis 18:12b NIV)

Based on "When God Seems Late" by Amy Carroll

Do you hear your disbelief and questions about God's timing echoed in Sarah's? *Now, Lord? I thought this would happen years ago. Aren't You just a little late?*

God answered Sarah's question in a way that answers ours, too. "Is anything too hard for the Lord? I will return to you at the appointed time next year, and Sarah will have a son" (Genesis 18:14).

Less than a year later, Isaac, the child whom God had promised 25 years before, was born. God was not late. His timing was perfect.

It may seem like God is slowing down your dreams, but He knows the entirety of your story from beginning to end. He also knows how your story weaves into the lives of others. We may be tapping our watches, but He is never late. He may seem slow, but He's always right on time. God Himself holds the appointed time in His hands.

Based on "When God Seems Late" by Amy Carroll

In the space below, write one thing you know to be true based off what you read today:

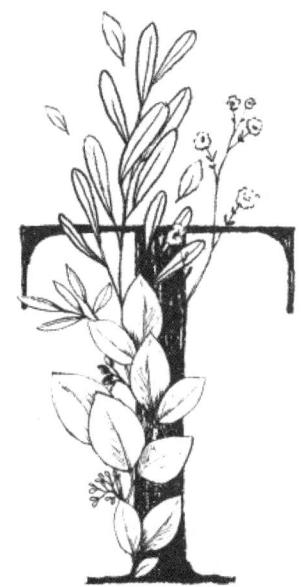

right now I need

TRUST

BLESSED ARE THOSE WHO TRUST IN THE LORD

"Blessed is the man who trusts in the Lord, whose trust is the Lord. He is like a tree planted by water, that sends out its roots by the stream, and does not fear when heat comes, for its leaves remain green, and is not anxious in the year of drought, for it does not cease to bear fruit." Jeremiah 17:7-8 (ESV)

Hard decisions. Financial burdens. Emotional uncertainty.

Sometimes it feels like life won't let up. We keep getting bad news, and we wonder why God is letting this happen to us. Does He really think we can go through all of this?

Maybe you are in a hard place today. Perhaps it's a place you've encountered before, and it's the last place you wanted to be. Here are a few things we can learn from Jeremiah's words:

First, Jeremiah reveals that we can be honest about how we feel.

Jeremiah doesn't paint a pretty picture with his words about what is taking place. Instead, he describes intense heat that withers everything around the tree. But he also points to a God who is close by. Our God knows what we are going through. He's our safe place.

Second, we can run to the life-giving source.

Based on "How Do I Trust Again?" by Suzie Eller

Hard places require wise choices. Hard places can make you feel empty. Yet there is a promise of refreshing that runs so deep that we are strengthened and nourished in spite of what is taking place.

Last, let's settle into this promise found in today's key verse: When we remain close to God in the hard places, there's fruit.

Fruit might come through joy that makes no sense in relation to circumstances.

Fruit can spring forth in laughter that erupts where darkness wants to take hold.

Fruit is planted inside of us as we hold tightly to a faith that is bigger than we are.

Push your roots deep in your trust in the Lord. Lean into God in the midst of drought, and see what fruit comes from your life as a result.

In the space below, write one thing you know to be true based off what you read today:

IF YOU BELIEVE, YOU WILL SEE

"Then Jesus said, 'Did I not tell you that if you believed, you would see the glory of God?'" John 11:40 (NIV)

Mary, Martha and their brother Lazarus were in Jesus' inner circle of friends. As part of the "in" crowd, Mary and Martha felt certain Jesus would come to them when Lazarus got sick. They had seen Jesus heal and minister to complete strangers, so of course He'd rush to those He loved! However, we see in John 11:4-6 that was not the case.

Jesus indeed loved Mary, Martha and Lazarus. Yet, even after He heard Lazarus was sick, He stayed where He was for two more days.

If Jesus loved His friends, why did He wait to go to their side? These verses appear to validate a fear of rejection: If Jesus ignored His friend Lazarus, will He ignore me too?

Trusting suddenly becomes too risky — we could get hurt again.

The truth is, when we experience emotional or physical trauma and God doesn't respond like we think He should, we have two choices: Either turn to God, trusting Him with the result, or run from God and become bitter. We can learn to trust again.

While others may let us down, we can trust that God will never let us down.

Based on "Learning to Trust Again" by Micca Campbell

Sickness, abuse and death are part of life in a fallen world that God will someday restore. Until then, God may allow you to go through hard things. It's not because He wants to punish you; it's because you may have something important to learn through the pain.

This was true with Mary and Martha. Jesus told Martha that she would see the glory of God if she believed. If we can choose to trust in the midst of fear, we will see the glory of God turn our pain into blessing.

As Mary and Martha believed, they witnessed the glory of God when He raised their brother from the dead. Their fears vanished and their faith was restored. If you and I want to exchange our fear for faith, we must believe that what Christ has in store for us is worth our present pain.

In the space below, write one thing you know to be true based off what you read today:

right now I need

HOPE

HOW LONG, LORD?

"My soul is in deep anguish. How long, Lord, how long?"
Psalm 6:3 (NIV)

When a diagnosis plunges us into the unknown; when the sting of rejection leaves us scarred and alone; when our best dreams shatter and fall apart; when fear imprisons and worries flood our heart ... we find ourselves wrestling with our questions in the darkness of disappointment and despair. And we wonder ...

Will peace ever trump this pain?

Will joy ever replace this sadness?

Will beauty ever grow from this brokenness?

Will morning ever come?

It's in these long nights of the soul where we can find great comfort in Scripture, especially the book of Psalms. Through these words, we peer into the hearts of other wrestling souls and hear the timeless echoes of our own impatient cries.

"My soul is in deep anguish. How long, Lord, how long?" (Psalm 6:3 NIV)

Based on "How to Hold on to Hope in the Dark" by Alicia Bruxvoort

"How long must I wrestle with my thoughts and day after day have sorrow in my heart? How long will my enemy triumph over me?" (Psalm 13:2 NIV)

But the psalms offer more than empathy when we've reached the end of our rope. These sacred words suggest a strategy for holding on to hope.

"Let the morning bring me word of your unfailing love, for I have put my trust in you. Show me the way I should go, for to you I entrust my life." (Psalm 143:8 NIV)

"But as for me, I will sing about your power. Each morning I will sing with joy about your unfailing love. For you have been my refuge, a place of safety when I am in distress." (Psalm 59:16 NLT)

God's Word reminds us that even when our circumstances sway, Christ's love remains the same (Romans 8:38-39). Though our faith may waver, His faithfulness won't. Hope flourishes when we shift our gaze from the darkness that surrounds us to the love that encircles us. And there, in the certainty of His love, we find peace for the present and strength for the days to come.

Based on "How to Hold on to Hope in the Dark" by Alicia Bruxvoort

In the space below, write one thing you know to be true based off what you read today:

I STILL DARE TO HOPE

"Yet I still dare to hope when I remember this ..."
Lamentations 3:21 (NLT)

Have you ever cried until tears no longer fell and your heart was broken in tiny pieces? Have you ever uttered, "Everything I hope for from the Lord is lost" Yes? Then you have something in common with the prophet Jeremiah.

Jeremiah, also known as the weeping prophet in the Old Testament, watched the temple of the Lord being burned to the ground by the Babylonians. Jeremiah's heart broke as the elements of the temple, such as the water basin and lamp snuffers, were stolen and taken to Babylon to be used to worship false gods. It was a hopeless situation.

In the midst of the devastation, Jeremiah prophesied God's words to the people of Judah and Jerusalem. Unfortunately, it wasn't good news. The Lord's immediate future for His people was one of discipline and the utter destruction of Jerusalem as well as His holy temple. Jeremiah was chosen by God to deliver these words to His people. Jeremiah did his job and did it well, but not without punishment, ridicule, insults and imprisonment by the recipients of the news.

Jeremiah shed tears until he said, "I have cried until the tears no longer come; my heart is broken" (Lamentations 2:11 NLT).

Based on "Dare to Hope" by Wendy Pope

His heart was broken for Jerusalem and for God's people, his people. In anguish Jeremiah lamented, "Everything I had hoped for from the Lord is lost" (Lamentations 3:18 NLT).

Then, in the midst of his despair, he dared. He dared to hope in what he remembered. Jeremiah remembered this about the Lord:

• His unfailing love

• His new mercies

• His never-ending faithfulness

• His inheritance

God's Word is just as alive and active today as it was in Jeremiah's day. It is designed to transform us from the inside out. Reading and applying its truths will redirect our perspective.

Are you in need of hope today? Will you choose to remember God's faithfulness, love and mercy, despite the despair and destruction around you? Today, dare to hope.

In the space below, write one thing you know to be true based off what you read today:

right now I need
PEACE

LET THE PEACE OF GOD RULE YOUR HEART

"Let the peace of Christ rule in your hearts, since as members of one body you were called to peace. And be thankful." Colossians 3:15 (NIV)

Have you ever heard the phrase, "There will never be any peace until we're all laid to rest"?

It's a relatable statement. Life is hard. And sometimes it's easy to despair over finding peace when trouble seems to lurk around every corner. When hard times come, many emotions can take over, and peace is probably the last emotion you feel.

Your peace is God's will. A peace that speaks of freedom from external pressures.

It's not something that comes and goes depending on our circumstances. Divine peace should govern our lives in all things at all times. When the things of life haunt us — that stack of bills, new tires for the car, anxious feelings of inadequacy — don't we long for peace?

Based on "True Peace Is Possible" by Micca Campbell

Here's the good news: We can have that kind of peace. Jesus told His disciples, "Peace I leave with you; my peace I give you. I do not give to you as the world gives. Do not let your hearts be troubled and do not be afraid" (John 14:27 NIV).

Jesus is not talking about the kind of peace we feel when a debt is finally paid. That's relief. It's not the kind of peace we experience when we can purchase that big house we've always wanted. That's gratification.

The peace Christ gives is fully satisfying. It's peace of mind, heart, body and soul. It's contentment knowing that no matter what happens, you are in the care of the Almighty.

The Bible has something to say about putting our trust in someone other than God: "Those who trust in themselves are fools, but those who walk in wisdom are kept safe" (Proverbs 28:26 NIV).

Resting in God's promises gives us the hope we need to stay focused on Him and His faithfulness, instead of on our circumstances. One way we can be certain we've really placed our trust in God is when we experience an indescribable peace.

Let this promise from the Lord in Isaiah 26:3 reassure you today, "You will keep in perfect peace those whose minds are steadfast, because they trust in you" (NIV).

Based on "True Peace Is Possible" by Micca Campbell

In the space below, write one thing you know to be true based off what you read today:

WHY DO YOU HIDE YOURSELF, LORD?

"Why, Lord, do you stand far off? Why do you hide yourself in times of trouble?" Psalm 10:1 (NIV)

If you've turned on your TV recently, you know there's always another news cycle to make you anxious. Stories of abuse, death, disaster, political corruption and a general lack of integrity are everywhere. And it can feel like things are getting worse instead of better.

Have you ever wondered what God would say if you asked Him, "God, what is going on in this world? And when are You going to do something about it?"

In Psalm 10, David wanted to know when God was going to step in and do something about the wickedness of the world. David prayed with a desperate heart, begging God's intervention and peace.

Maybe you've felt that way too. Maybe you're not only overwhelmed by what's happening in the world, but by what is going on inside of you. The stress never seems to go away, and you feel as if God is far away, not intervening to help.

Based on "Living in a World Gone Wrong" by Tracie Miles

In prayer, David voiced his deepest fears and honest feelings. He solicited God's wisdom for greater understanding, yet surrendered to trusting that God sees all, knows all and would handle it all when the time was right.

Our world has gone wrong due to the existence of sin, but we have a choice in how we respond. Instead of letting despair pull us further from God, or cause us to doubt His goodness, we can choose to lean on our faith and draw closer to Him instead, just like David.

Let's choose to proclaim God's sovereignty today, trust in His ways and be a voice for His truths even when the ways of this world break our hearts.

Based on "Living in a World Gone Wrong" by Tracie Miles

In the space below, write one thing you know to be true based off what you read today:

right now I need

BALANCE

LORD, YOU ALONE ARE MY PORTION

"Lord, you alone are my portion and my cup; you make my lot secure. The boundary lines have fallen for me in pleasant places; surely I have a delightful inheritance." Psalm 16:5-6 (NIV)

Have you ever lived in a season without a pause button? Maybe you're in that season right now, and you're realizing that unless life starts to slow down, things will fall apart. But it also begs the question: Does life balance even exist?

For most of us, there are few non-negotiable boundaries when it comes to busyness. We live without the built-in rhythms of the rising and setting sun that guided our ancestors just a few generations back. Few of us live an agricultural or pastoral life led by the gentle demands of animals and crops.

We could work 24 hours a day if our bodies and minds would let us. Hence, we get drawn into a nonstop lifestyle of work.

While the Bible honors hard work, it does not say we need to be busy all the time. This is where we need wisdom to find a balance between work and rest. King David acknowledges God's plans perfectly in one of his psalms:

"Lord, you alone are my portion and my cup; you make my lot secure. The boundary lines have fallen for me in pleasant places; surely I have a delightful inheritance" (Psalm 16:5-6 NIV).

Although David refers to property lines, this is a lovely image of God's plan for balancing our lives. He never meant for our lives to be a jumble of overcommitment. Rather, God's plan is peaceful and ordered. And in order to find that pleasant place, we need to have healthy boundaries on our time with lots of margin built in.

By creating balance in establishing boundaries for our busyness, we give ourselves breathing room. We give ourselves time to think, dream and plan. Busy gets seriously out-of-control without boundaries.

Finding balance is possible. Establishing healthy boundaries involves editing the content in our lives, carefully identifying what's most important ... what God is asking us to do today. Then as we remove what's not ours to do, we can breathe a sigh of relief at the beauty that's revealed in our lives.

In the space below, write one thing you know to be true based off what you read today:

SEEK FIRST THE KINGDOM

"Therefore do not be anxious, saying, 'What shall we eat?' or 'What shall we drink?' or 'What shall we wear?' For the Gentiles seek after all these things, and your heavenly Father knows that you need them all. But seek first the kingdom of God and his righteousness, and all these things will be added to you." Matthew 6:31-33 (ESV)

Do you wear a lot of hats? During the course of a busy week you may wear any of these hats: counselor, co-worker, daughter, sister, friend, wife, mother, aunt, grandma, neighbor, chef, nurse, referee, committee chair, and oh, yeah … a woman of God.

It's easy to misplace our identity in such roles. And sadly for many Christ-followers, often the last hat we place on top is the crown we wear as a daughter of the King of Kings.

Jesus gives simple, straight-shooting words in Matthew 6:33. Without being complex, He tells us gently, but firmly, what must be done to meet the many demands in our lives and yet still help our hearts not to worry: "But seek first the kingdom of God and his righteousness, and all these things will be added to you."

As a result of buying into a keep-moving mindset, we have practically no white space left on our calendars.

Based on "Wearing Too Many Hats" by Karen Ehman

Our kids are carted from one activity to the next, and many families hardly eat dinner together anymore. Something in us longs to "do more" by painting our lives in a bright, bold shade of busy.

While our unfinished tasks may tempt us to fret, Christ stands whispering … *Stop. Halt the hustle. Resist the rush. Press pause to find a little calm in the chaos. Seek first My kingdom and My righteousness, and all of these things will be given to you as well.*

Perhaps His words will prompt us to do a little hat-reduction, ridding our schedules of some of the activities that clamor for our attention, unsettle our souls and draw us away from time spent with Him.

Whatever set of hats God directs you to keep wearing, remember to don them in proper order. They will only stay standing when you place the crown you wear as a daughter of the King of Kings on first!

Based on "Wearing Too Many Hats" by Karen Ehman

In the space below, write one thing you know to be true based off what you read today:

right now I need

PERSPECTIVE

A NEW NAME

"And as her soul was departing (for she was dying), she called his name Ben-oni; but his father called him Benjamin." Genesis 35:18 (ESV)

What will it take for you, at the end of your life, to be able to say, "It is well with my soul"?

In our key verse today, we're witnesses to the ending of a story. The comparison-filled journey of two sisters, Rachel and Leah, ended in a very sad, sorrowful place: "And as her soul was departing (for she was dying), she called his name Ben-oni; but his father called him Benjamin" (Genesis 35:18).

An unexpected death.

Rachel's life ends while giving birth to a son. And with her last words, she gave her son the name "Ben-oni," which means "son of my sorrow." Things were not well with her soul. And her name choice reveals the depth of hurt and pain within her.

But her husband Jacob (whose own name eventually became Israel), decided to give their son a new name: Benjamin. Which meant "son of my right hand, a place of high favor." His son would not live his life with a name representing sorrow.

Based on "Give It a New Name" by Nicki Koziarz

No one knows why God allows things to happen the way they do. Jacob most likely struggled with this, too — wondering as his beloved wife slipped into eternity and he held that baby boy.

At some point, we'll all find ourselves wading through unexpected pain or struggle. But there's a God who gives us a love that redefines our dry seasons.

His Son Jesus is the best example of how God can take pain and rename it something powerful. Like the meaning of Benjamin's new name, Jesus, after a sorrowful season, now sits at the right hand of His Father (Ephesians 1:20-23).

His sorrow was a sacrifice on the cross, which changed everything for us. And because of Jesus, we can walk through hard places and still say, "It is well with my soul."

It doesn't mean we'll do it perfectly, smoothly or even with a smile on our faces. But it means we trust God so much we believe He can rename even the hardest of situations and turn them into something of eternal value.

Trust God with your pain, and He'll continue to write you a new story.

Based on "Give It a New Name" by Nicki Koziarz

In the space below, write one thing you know to be true based off what you read today:

INTENDED FOR GOOD

"You intended to harm me, but God intended it all for good."
Genesis 50:20a (NLT)

Sometimes life feels unfair. Everything seems to go wrong for us. We didn't sign up to go through all this, did we?

A young man in Scripture, Joseph, also found himself smack-dab in a heap of hassles and difficult situations he never signed up for. His jealous brothers sold him into slavery. He was whisked away to live in a foreign land. To top it off, he was falsely accused of raping his master's wife even though he tried his best to stay away from her. He even wound up in prison.

These unjust circumstances could have had him complaining, "I didn't sign up for this!" He could have retaliated against those who had caused his turmoil. But he didn't.

Joseph maintained a God-fearing, God-honoring attitude throughout his ordeals, even as a slave with no freedom in sight.

At the end of his life, we get a glimpse into his continual Christ-like behavior. He'd risen from slave to governor of Egypt through his discernment and wisdom.

Based on "I Didn't Sign Up for This" by Karen Ehman

When his brothers came to buy grain from the Egyptian authorities during a famine, they were shocked to see their younger brother — long thought dead — sitting in a position of power. They feared he would retaliate for the cruel things they did to him, but Joseph's response? "You intended to harm me, but God intended it all for good" (Genesis 50:20a).

Joseph refused to let life knock him off course and prevent him from living a life that pleased God. He believed in a God who works all things together for good. By recognizing God's redemption of horrific circumstances, he found true spiritual freedom from self-pity, anger and retaliation. Instead, he characterized what God wants of us in Micah 6:8b, "And what does the Lord require of you but to do justice, to love kindness, and to walk humbly with your God?" (NASB)

Could we dare to get our eyes off our sometimes minor problems and spend time doing justice, acting kindly and humbly walking with God?

No matter our circumstances, it's never too late to be free. Our God-honoring attitude that comes from a shift in perspective can help us find spiritual freedom. And our intentional actions can help others imprisoned in slavery find freedom, physically, spiritually and emotionally.

Based on "I Didn't Sign Up for This" by Karen Ehman

In the space below, write one thing you know to be true based off what you read today:

....
....
....
....
....
....
....
....
....
....
....
....
....
....
....
....
....
....
....

right now I need

CONTENTMENT

NEVER THIRST AGAIN

"Jesus answered, 'Everyone who drinks this water will be thirsty again, but whoever drinks the water I give them will never thirst. Indeed, the water I give them will become in them a spring of water welling up to eternal life.'" John 4:13-14 (NIV)

Have you ever wanted something different for your life, but you just didn't know what that different thing was? The Samaritan woman at the well had the same problem. She wanted something different. She was thirsty and didn't even know what she was thirsty for.

We all come into the world spiritually thirsty. After the nourishing umbilical cord is severed, we begin our journey to discover living water to satisfy the soul. Oh, we don't know it yet, but God's placed the desire for something more in every one of His image bearers.

Until we meet Jesus, we fumble about trying to quench the God-given thirst with anything and anyone who offers temporary relief. But it's just that — temporary.

It is only in a relationship with Jesus that we discover what we're all truly longing for.

We've all been like the Samaritan woman — drinking from shallow streams. Maybe not the same shallow stream, but unsatisfying ones nonetheless.

Based on "I'd Be Happy If..." by Sharon Jaynes

All of them leave us thirsty for more — or at least for something different. Jesus offers us what He offered her: freely flowing, refreshing water from the indwelling Holy Spirit that quenches every thirst, washes away every sin and flows into every nook and cranny of our beings.

It's like being near a lake. I can look at the lake, swim in the lake, even stand in the lake and still die of thirst. The only way for the water to enter my system is to actually drink it.

Likewise, we can read about Jesus, hear sermons about Jesus, even believe He was a good man. But until we actually believe Jesus is God's Son, the Messiah, who died for our sins and rose again, until we partake of Jesus and make Him Lord of our lives, we'll remain thirsty.

"I'll be happy if ..."

How would you finish that sentence? If you had a man? A baby? A bigger house? A smaller waistline? If it's anything other than a personal, growing, intimate relationship with Jesus, your water bucket will remain riddled with holes.

Today, let's fill our buckets and drink deeply.

Based on "I'd Be Happy If ..." by Sharon Jaynes

In the space below, write one thing you know to be true based off what you read today:

FORGET NOT HIS BENEFITS

"Praise the Lord, my soul, and forget not all his benefits…"
Psalm 103:2 (NIV)

God has created a place of safety for you within His Word. His commandments are designed to protect you, not restrict you. God gives us the good gifts of His mercy, grace and forgiveness to remind us to stay near. He pours His love on us and draws us deep into His family.

Below is a verse from the well-known hymn, *Come Thou Fount:*

O to grace how great a debtor

Daily I'm constrained to be!

Let Thy goodness, like a fetter

Bind my wandering heart to Thee.

Prone to wander, Lord, I feel it.

Prone to leave the God I love.

Here's my heart, O take and seal it,

Seal it for Thy courts above.

Based on "Prone to Wander" by Amy Carroll

Even though God pours out His love on us, our hearts are still prone to wander. We ignore His truth and make decisions that launch us outside the safety of His guidelines. We harbor wrong thoughts. These choices can take us away from God's heart. And yet He longs to draw us home again.

The opening verses of Psalm 103 provide a key to keep our wandering hearts close to God: "Praise the Lord, my soul; all my inmost being, praise his holy name. Praise the Lord, my soul, and forget not all his benefits" (Psalm 103:1-2 NIV).

By praising God and rehearsing His benefits, we can train our hearts to find contentment close to God, rather than far from Him.

When we want to wander, the verses that follow Psalm 103:1-2 list even more reasons to praise and thank God.

God's love for you means He will keep pursuing you and finding ways to keep you near Him. Let's join with the Lord in staying in the protective boundary lines He's given us by praising and rehearsing His faithful ways. Doing so will bind our wandering hearts to God and keep us safe in the nurturing places He's created for you and me.

In the space below, write one thing you know to be true based off what you read today:

right now I need
PERSEVERANCE

WE NEVER GIVE UP

"Therefore, since God in his mercy has given us this new way, we never give up." 2 Corinthians 4:1 (NLT)

Maybe for reasons only you and God know, you've found yourself saying "I can't take anymore." Maybe giving up hope about that difficult situation, problem or relationship seems easier than hanging onto it.

Maybe you're a single parent, and financial worries coupled with the emotional weight of parenting and being alone feels overwhelming ...

Maybe you try to live frugally, yet money never seems to stretch far enough ...

Maybe you're unhappy at your job, but no other opportunities have arisen ...

Maybe your heart longs for a husband, but you're tired of the dating game ...

Maybe your circumstances feel out-of-control and change seems hopeless ...

Sometimes it feels easier to just give up.

In 2 Corinthians 4, Paul reminded the church at Corinth that they each held a treasure in their heart — the Spirit of God — which was the sole reason they could persevere when they felt like quitting in the face of adversities, especially when it came to defending the gospel.

Based on "Give Up or God Up" by Tracie Miles

We see proof that although he stumbled, Paul consistently focused on God. Every time Paul wanted to give up, he chose to God-up instead. He chose to depend on God's power and strength instead of his own. He suffered mental and spiritual exhaustion in addition to physical pain, hunger, thirst and difficult living conditions. That's enough to make anyone want to give up! Yet despite his weakest moments, he never did.

Everyone struggles with wanting to give up at times. But like Paul, the moment we catch ourselves feeling that way, we can choose to give up or God-up.

We can let our thoughts and feelings deplete us of strength, hope and joy, or we can lean fully into God and ask for Him to carry us in our weakest moments.

Based on "Give Up or God Up" by Tracie Miles

In the space below, write one thing you know to be true based off what you read today:

....
....
....
....
....
....
....
....
....
....
....
....
....
....
....
....
....
....
....
....

THE WILL OF HIM WHO SENT ME

"'My food,' said Jesus, 'is to do the will of him who sent me and to finish his work.'" John 4:34 (NIV)

Starting a project can be fun and exciting. Optimism always abounds at the beginning of something new.

But what seemed fun at first eventually becomes hard work. Then discouragement sets in. Perfectionist tendencies stifle moving forward. And it's easy to give up rather than finish what we started.

Finishing well requires discipline that doesn't come naturally. But it's key to living a life that's manageable and reflects God's priorities for us. So while our shelves may include books on time management and productivity, the best role model of finishing well is Jesus.

Jesus is the picture of focus and discipline, especially in the midst of many people demanding His attention. In the book of John, we read a story about Jesus sitting by a well while His disciples went for food. As He waited, a solitary woman came to draw water and Jesus engaged her in a life-changing conversation — not only for her but for her entire village.

Based on "Finish What You Start" by Glynnis Whitwer

On this day, Jesus could have pleaded exhaustion or frustration. He'd been traveling, it was warm and He was hungry. One of those challenges would have been enough to derail me. Instead, Jesus narrowed His focus on one woman and finished the assignment God gave Him.

After reuniting with His disciples, they tried to get Jesus to eat. He responded: "'My food,' said Jesus, 'is to do the will of him who sent me and to finish his work'" (John 4:34 NIV).

Jesus knew what His Father had asked Him to do and was committed to "finish" this work. In this passage, Jesus models clarity of purpose, perseverance and compassion — all characteristics we want.

If you feel like you are always starting things and never finishing, perhaps it would help to focus on only one or two things God is calling you to today. Don't try and tackle everything at once. Ask God for His priorities for your life, and concentrate on doing your best in those areas.

Changing lifelong patterns of not finishing things will take time. When we submit our overwhelmed feelings to God, He'll give us the strength to persevere.

Based on "Finish What You Start" by Glynnis Whitwer

In the space below, write one thing you know to be true based off what you read today:

right now I need

REASSURANCE

THE WAY OF THE RIGHTEOUS

"The path of the righteous is level; you, the Upright One, make the way of the righteous smooth." Isaiah 26:7 (NIV)

Have you ever sought God's direction, followed His lead, only to find yourself walking a path marked by concerns that cause you to stumble?

God often calls us to step out into something uncertain, but sometimes the potholes in our path make us wonder if we are really on the right road. Unanswered, difficult questions can make us doubt the direction we've been given. Did we hear God wrong?

In the book of Exodus, after Moses and the Israelites fled slavery in Egypt, they were quickly chased down by Pharaoh and his army, "The Egyptians—all Pharaoh's horses and chariots, horsemen and troops—pursued the Israelites and overtook them as they camped by the sea near Pi Hahiroth, opposite Baal Zephon" (Exodus 14:9).

The Israelites were suddenly terrified. They had come all this way, believing the Lord would set them free from their captors, only to be overtaken by their enemy, "They said to Moses, 'Was it because there were no graves in Egypt that you brought us to the desert to die? What have you done to us by bringing us out of Egypt? Didn't we say to you in Egypt, "Leave us alone; let us serve the Egyptians"? It would have been better for us to serve the Egyptians than to die in the desert!'" (Exodus 14:11-12)

Based on "When Potholes Fill Your Path" by Alicia Bruxvoort

Their cries may sound crazy to us, but we've all felt this way at some point or another — it can be more comfortable to stay in less-than-ideal circumstances, rather than to risk everything by taking a new path.

Sometimes we need reassurance. The Israelites certainly did, "Moses answered the people, 'Do not be afraid. Stand firm and you will see the deliverance the Lord will bring you today. The Egyptians you see today you will never see again. The Lord will fight for you; you need only to be still'" (Exodus 14:13-14).

You've probably heard the next part of the story, because it's almost unbelievable: God parts the Red Sea, giving Moses and the Israelites their path to deliverance. To freedom.

Whatever the path looks like, God has a plan for every step. We may be trekking toward a new school year or stepping into an empty nest; stumbling along a painful detour or skipping into a new job; but no matter where we're headed, God is aware of every gap in the road He's established for us, and He will give you a way through.

Based on "When Potholes Fill Your Path" by Alicia Bruxvoort

In the space below, write one thing you know to be true based off what you read today:

A SURE AND STEADFAST ANCHOR

"We who have fled for refuge might have strong encouragement to hold fast to the hope set before us. We have this as a sure and steadfast anchor of the soul." Hebrews 6:18b-19a (ESV)

In Luke 8, Jesus and His disciples were sailing in a boat, and Jesus fell asleep. While He was sleeping, a storm came down on the lake. As the boat filled with water, they wondered why Jesus continued to sleep and didn't respond to the raging storm as quickly as they wanted.

The disciples feared the potential outcome of the storm. They pleaded with Jesus to help them — and He did (Luke 8:24 ESV).

When we spend a lot of time worrying, it may be a sign that we have misplaced our trust. When the storms rage and the winds blow, and they will, is our faith in Jesus, or in the outcome of our circumstances?

If we compare ourselves to a ship and the hardships of life to storms, then hope is the anchor that keeps us from being shipwrecked. But an anchor is dependent on two things: the cable that tethers it to the ship, and the solid ground.

The cable connecting us to hope is faith … an assurance of Jesus' love, goodness and power. Our faith believes He still speaks to storms and with a word, can calm them. Faith is being confident that His promises will carry us through this life safely into an eternity spent with Him. Now that's hopeful!

Based on "When the Storms Rage and the Winds Blow" by Sharon Glasgow

And the ground to which our anchors need to be fixed? That is Jesus. He is firm and unchanging. As the waves rise and the winds howl, sometimes it's tempting to pull away from Him, especially when we ask, "Why?" But storms are opportunities to dig deeper into our relationship with Jesus through reading and memorizing Scripture, praying to and worshipping Him.

The storms will rage, and the winds will blow. But to believe in the middle of it all, to have faith that leads to hope in Jesus, that's the secret to riding out the storms in life.

Today, if circumstances and worry are tossing you about, cast your anchor of hope into Jesus and pray for the faith to believe His promises are true. He is powerful enough to calm your storms and keep you safe.

Based on "When the Storms Rage and the Winds Blow" by Sharon Glasgow

In the space below, write one thing you know to be true based off what you read today:

ENCOURAGEMENT FOR TODAY
Daily Devotions

What does the Bible say about what you're going through?

Subscribe to our FREE *Encouragement for Today* daily devotions to receive daily, biblical encouragement that will help you filter everyday life through the truth of God's Word.

Go to www.proverbs31.org/devotions to sign up for **free!**

ABOUT PROVERBS 31 MINISTRIES

She is clothed with strength and dignity; she can laugh at the days to come.

PROVERBS 31:25

Proverbs 31 Ministries is a nondenominational, nonprofit Christian ministry that seeks to lead women into a personal relationship with Christ. With Proverbs 31:10-31 as a guide, Proverbs 31 Ministries reaches women in the middle of their busy days through free devotions, daily radio messages, speaking events, conferences, resources, online Bible studies and training in the call to write, speak and lead others.

We are real women offering real-life solutions to those striving to maintain life's balance, in spite of today's hectic pace and cultural pull away from godly principles.

Wherever a woman may be on her spiritual journey, Proverbs 31 Ministries exists to be a trusted friend who understands the challenges she faces and walks by her side, encouraging her as she walks toward the heart of God.

Visit us online today at proverbs31.org!